The Quilt

and the Poetry of Alabama Music

Frye Gaillard & Kathryn Scheldt

Solomon & George, Publisher
414 South Gay Street
Auburn, Alabama 36830

All song lyrics previously published by Shellkat Enterprises, (BMI)
and In Sync Music (BMI).
Reprinted here with permission. All songs available at
www.kathrynscheldt.com

Portions of Frye Gaillard's essays appeared in different form in
The Americana Gazette and *Mobile Bay Monthly*. Gaillard has
written extensively about Hank Williams and Emmylou Harris in
his earlier books, *Watermelon Wine: Remembering the Golden
Years of Country Music; The Heart of Dixie: Southern Rebels,
Renegades and Heroes; and With Music and Justice for All: Some
Southerners and Their Passions.*

ISBN 978-0-9853404-1-4

Cover art by Nall

Cover and book design by Corinna Herndon Ray

Editors, Jay Lamar and Rachael Fowler

Published with the Support of the HISTORY MUSEUM OF MOBILE

Table of Contents

Part I – The Poetry of Alabama Music

Reflections by Frye Gaillard

Georgiana

On the dusty main street of Georgiana, Alabama, the Ga-Ana Theater looks as if it's seen better days – and in fact, it has. Among other things, it's the place where Hank Williams, a native of Georgiana, delivered one of his early performances, and though the brick exterior looks faded and old, it is, for a handful of artists in the know, a historic stop on the country music circuit.

A few years ago, the headliner for the first show I'd ever seen there was the Grand Ole Opry's George Hamilton IV, a legend in his own right, who was paying tribute to Georgiana's most famous son. Before the hometown folk, the hardest of hard-core Hank Williams fans, Hamilton ran through a sampling of Hank's hits and a few of his lesser known gospel numbers, and then introduced his special guest for the evening. He was performing that night with Kathryn Scheldt, an Alabama songwriter who opened her set with something she had only recently recorded.

"Rufus and Hank," co-written by Scheldt in memory of Williams, was also a tribute to Rufus Payne, an African-American street singer who had been the musical mentor to a teenaged Hank.

Made a funny pair down by the railroad track

Skinny white boy and his friend who was black

In rural Alabama in the 1930s, it was borderline scandalous for a rough and hard-living man of the streets, especially if he was black, to be hanging out with a young white boy. But as music historians are quick to tell you the music that Payne and Williams made together left a permanent impression on Hank, infusing his country sound with the blues.

I knew as I listened to Scheldt in Georgiana that this was a writer who understood such things, and without a lot of fanfare, was doing her part to keep that musical tradition alive. Already, I had seen her career evolve over the course of four well-crafted CDs. I had heard her play in listening rooms and other grass-roots venues throughout the South, and had even written a few songs with her, having discovered a kindred Americana spirit.

The lyrics of some of those songs are included in the pages of this book. But as we assembled them for publication, Kathryn and I agreed that it was appropriate – essential, even – to pay tribute to the poetry of Alabama music.

We knew we needed to start with Hank Williams, so we headed north one morning on I-65, turning off at Georgiana, to mingle once again with the ghosts. You can feel them there in the half-empty streets, and in the rambling, wood-frame house that is now a museum, dedicated to keeping Williams' memory alive. As a frail and sickly teenaged boy he had lived in that house with his domineering mother, Miss Lillie, who took in boarders and according to local rumors, some of them unkind, did whatever it took to survive. Hank's father by then was living in a mental hospital, a shell-shocked victim of World War I, and the desperate loneliness of those days drove Hank's first forays into poetry.

The dad I've got, you see, he comes but once a year
I ask him why he stayed away and he said lookie here,
and tried to take my mind away by pulling at my ear
Mom wasn't there, she never is when Papa pays a call

When she came back I tried to talk, but Mom said that's all

Paul Hemphill, one of Williams' biographers, called those lines "a piece of doggerel," and perhaps they are. But they are also a cry from the heart, clear and direct, the foreshadowing from a troubled boyhood of what was to come. The fundamental truth about Hank's life was that it never got any better. Before he died at the age of twenty-nine, he lived in constant physical pain, the result of a deformity in his spine, and it was one of the things that drove him to drink. But there was also the matter of his lovesick blues – his yearning for a father, his resentments toward an overbearing mother, and his turbulent, sometimes violent marriage to a woman with whom he was desperately in love.

Whatever else you can say about Audrey Williams, a wife whose fidelity he had reason to doubt – and whom he once attempted to shoot – she clearly inspired some very good songs. In the rural South, a world that in the 1930s and '40s was already overflowing with pain, devastated by the Great Depression, Hank gave people a way to let it out. In some of his songs, particularly the gospel numbers he recorded under the name of Luke the Drifter, he wrote precociously about ethical issues that would emerge over time – the double standards imposed upon women, the overlooked wisdom of African Americans – but mostly he wrote about broken hearts.

On June 11, 1949, he made his debut at the Grand Ole Opry, choosing a song, uncharacteristically, that he didn't write. But his rendition that night of "Lovesick Blues," with his yodeling moan about being lo-o-onesome, was so unique it was like he had written the whole thing from scratch. They say he encored six or seven times, singing the same song over and over, and the people who had packed the Ryman Auditorium apparently could not get enough.

Whatever his talents onstage, however – and when he was sober he was one of the best – Hank was even more gifted as a songwriter. Some critics didn't think so at first. The words he chose were simple enough, about what you would expect from a country boy from rural Alabama – a man without much formal education. If his lyrics were uncomplicated, however, the emotions they sought to capture were not. In one of Williams' best-known songs, "Cold, Cold Heart," the central character yearns for the love of a woman out of reach. She is still hung up on another man, one who has clearly done her wrong, and the singer hurts for her unhappiness as well – clinging in iambic meter to a question he simply can't shove aside:

Why can't I free your doubtful mind and melt your cold, cold heart?

As Hank once said about another of his songs, "It's not too bad for an Alabama hillbilly." Subtle as it was, however, "Cold, Cold Heart" was not Hank's best. That distinction almost certainly goes to a song he wrote with his producer, Fred Rose. "I'm So Lonesome I Could Cry" consists of sixteen lines of metaphor and imagery that comprise, not the story line of an old-fashioned ballad, or even a typical Hank Williams lament, but rather the haunting word picture of an abstract feeling.

The silence of a falling star lights up a purple sky, and as I wonder where you are I'm so lonesome I could cry.

In an earlier book, *Watermelon Wine: The Spirit of Country Music*, I wanted to write about those lines and why they work, and this was about as close as I could come: "The metaphor of a sky being lit by silence is precisely the way it strikes the brain – hearing and sight are at work simultaneously, blended at the moment of perception. And there are the smaller things. The sky is purple instead of dark, black, or something more obvious, and there is the subjunctive verb in the title of the song – the singer isn't crying, but he could – which suggests a kind of strength and endurance that is all the more lonesome because the feeling is bottled inside."

In the end, of course, such analysis falls far short of the lyrics, and this is the heart of the Hank Williams legacy. He raised the poetic bar for country music.

There were also – and this was critically important as well – the lessons learned from Rufus Payne, who, in the 1930s, sang his songs by the railroad tracks, and taught young Hank how to play to a crowd. Their relationship was admittedly double-edged, for Payne was known around Georgiana as Tee-Tot, a reference to the fact that while he sang he often sipped from a jar of iced tea, laced inevitably with something alcoholic. It soon became apparent that even as a boy Hank possessed a desperate affinity for such brew, and Tee-Tot, his mentor and friend, may, inadvertently, have nudged him on a path to alcoholic ruin.

Certainly, that is where Hank ended up. On August 11, 1952, despite the fact that he was the most popular performer in country music, he was fired from his job at the Grand Ole Opry. The executives there were simply fed up, having lost all tolerance for his binging, the nights when Hank was too wasted to sing, and sometimes failed to show up at all.

"Hank was an alcoholic," said his friend, Jerry Rivers, the fiddle player in his band. "When he produced and wrote songs and made a little money and was feeling successful, he managed to control it. But sooner or later, he'd be drinking again, and Hank couldn't write his name when he was drunk. He couldn't crawl onstage, and the people at the Opry just lost patience with him."

After his firing it was all downhill. On December 31, 1952, he was lying drunk in the backseat of a Cadillac, headed north to Canton, Ohio, for a show scheduled on New Year's Day. Shortly after midnight, with the snow falling hard, Hank's young driver, Charles Carr, pulled off the road in Oak Hill, West Virginia, planning to grab a cup of coffee. He glanced at Hank, who was sprawled in the back, and suddenly realized there was no sign of life. He rushed to the Pure Oil station nearby, asking frantically for directions to the hospital, but it was too late. Hank Williams was dead at the age of twenty-nine, and the people who knew him were not surprised. He had simply been living too hard to survive.

Remarkably, however, the ugly morbidity of Hank Williams' life has receded to a secondary place in his legend. He is remembered most urgently – and among country music fans, that is not too strong a word – for his stunning body of work: songs with lyrics so beautifully crafted that in 2010 they won him a posthumous Pulitzer Prize. And there was Rufus Payne. This nearly forgotten musician of the streets, who died in obscurity in 1939, had bequeathed to Hank his understanding of the blues, that musical alchemy in which hard times are converted into something a human being can bear.

Over in Tuskegee, while Rufus and Hank were making their music in Georgiana, an African-American author by the name of Albert Murray was beginning a lifelong study of such things. At Booker T. Washington's Tuskegee Institute, Murray was an avid student of literature, but he says he came to believe over time that music and literature were joined at the heart.

"Life is a low-down dirty shame …" Murray once wrote, in an extended essay on the blues. "We do not receive wisdom. We must discover it for ourselves, after a journey through the wilderness that no one else can make for us, that no one can spare us, for our wisdom is the point of view from which we have come at last to view the world."

As Murray understood it, all of us share with the musicians among us the opportunity to find a meaning in the journey, and by an act of poetic will – an emulation of the blues – to transform the pain of life into beauty and strength.

Not long ago, as I was reading Murray's words, I thought of a song co-written by a friend of mine, Rick Hirsch, guitarist for the southern rock band Wet Willie. The group had roots in Alabama, having come together in Mobile, before blazing a trail across the musical landscape. In 1974, their biggest record, "Keep on Smilin'," made it to number ten on the Billboard charts. It was a song written primarily by lead singer Jimmy Hall, with Hirsch and other members of the band adding bits and pieces here and there. This was the heart of what they had to say:

Keep on smilin' through the rain, laughin' at the pain
Rollin' with the changes til the sun comes out again

As Hank Williams might have understood well – even though offstage he could never live up to such a noble demand – this was the hope and poetry of the blues.

Florence, Sheffield, and Muscle Shoals

Hank was not the first in Alabama's lineage of great musicians to reach across the racial divide. A half century earlier there was W. C. Handy.

Handy, "the Father of the Blues," was born in 1873 in a log cabin home in the town of Florence. He became a master of music theory, an admirer of the European composers – artists like Mozart and Beethoven, who wrote with such facility and grace. But he was also a devotee of the blues, the music of ordinary African Americans, who sang in styles full of subtlety and feeling.

"The primitive southern Negro, as he sang," Handy wrote, "was sure to bear down on the third and seventh tone of the scale, slurring between major and minor… I tried to convey this effect … by introducing flat thirds and sevenths (now called blue notes) into my song…."

Later, in Memphis, where he moved in 1909, Handy established a publishing company, featuring the work of blues musicians, which helped legitimize the artistry of that form. Very importantly, he also began to publish white artists, for music, he thought, could be the universal reprieve from the racism that he saw all around.

A generation later, Sam Phillips, another native of

Florence, emphatically shared that article of faith. Phillips, who was white, was born in 1923, a tenant farmer's son who toiled in the cotton fields of Alabama side by side with black farm workers. In the 1940s, he worked as a deejay at WLAY radio in Muscle Shoals, a town close to Florence, and the thing he liked about the station was its open format. It played black music, as well as white, those great and parallel traditions in the South, and Phillips saw potential in that choice.

In 1950, he opened a recording studio in Memphis, producing such rhythm and blues icons as Howlin' Wolf, Rufus Thomas, and Bobby Blue Bland. All the while, he was hoping he could find a white singer with the same kind of soul. Then in 1954, Elvis Presley walked through his door. They soon cut a record with Arthur Crudup's "That's All Right, Mama," a delta blues song, on one side – and on the other, Bill Monroe's bluegrass standard, "Blue Moon of Kentucky." Elvis sang the black song white and the white song black, and some say rock 'n' roll was born at that moment.

Even Phillips' most rabid critics – and they were suddenly abundant – knew that something fundamental had changed. This was the same year the United States Supreme Court declared segregated schools unconstitutional, and members of the White Citizens Council, among other segregationists, were driven to a dual kind of frenzy. They hated rock 'n' roll, hated Sam Phillips and Elvis Presley, as vehemently as they hated the U.S. Supreme Court. This was "jungle music," they declared, the first step on the road to "mongrelization," and there was a kernel of truth at the heart of their rage. Cultural barriers were breaking down, and music was on the cutting edge of the change.

This became even clearer a few years later in Florence, when a group of white musicians – Rick Hall, Billy Sherrill, and Tom Stafford – opened another recording studio. In 1961, Hall produced a song called "You Better Move On," written and sung by Arthur Alexander, a black songwriter from nearby Sheffield. Slowly, over time, Alexander, who worked for much of his life as a bus driver, was recognized as one of America's iconic songwriters. He was part country, part blues, both in the way he sang and the way he wrote. His songs told stories, often with multi-layered emotions; the protagonist, for example, in an Alexander song called "Anna" is deeply in love but willing to let his woman go if she can find greater happiness with another man.

Hall took the money he made with Alexander and opened FAME studios in Muscle Shoals, which quickly became one of the great recording centers in the country. Alabama artists such as Percy Sledge ("When a Man Loves a Woman"), Wilson Pickett ("Mustang Sally"), and Clarence Carter ("Slip Away" and "Patches") cut major hits in Muscle Shoals, and the remarkable thing about it was this: The musicians who backed these superb black singers were, almost without exception, white.

"We were like brothers," remembered Percy Sledge, "like family. We were as one."

Such is the heart of the Muscle Shoals story, an interracial legacy that changed the sound and face of southern music. But there was another dimension as well, lesser known perhaps, yet equally important. This particular corner of northern Alabama also became a songwriter's mecca. Arthur Alexander set the tone (the only artist ever to write for the Beatles, Bob Dylan, and the Rolling Stones), and he was soon followed by Dan Penn and Spooner Oldham, who wrote an impressive string of hits. Penn and Oldham were both white – small-town boys who loved the sweet soul music of home.

Some of the songs they wrote were simply fun, including "Cry Like a Baby," a 1960s hit for the Box Tops. But other songs probed the human heart. With Memphis songwriter Chips Moman, Penn wrote "Dark End of the Street," a song about illicit love recorded initially by James Carr, and later by Emmylou Harris and Linda Ronstadt. He also wrote "Do Right Woman, Do Right Man," recorded first by Aretha Franklin, and then Willie Nelson, demonstrating again that black and white music were deeply intertwined.

More than twenty years later, in 1993, another young writer came to Muscle Shoals. Among music historians, Kate Campbell has not yet achieved the renown of Dan Penn, nor have her songs become major hits. But Campbell may well be the most literary songwriter ever to ply her trade in Alabama. She actually grew up in Mississippi, not far from the delta town of Sledge, home of Charley Pride, and as a girl in the early 1970s she remembers hearing his sunburned voice, singing "Kiss an Angel Good Morning" on the radio. She loved country music from the very start. Her heroes were Emmylou Harris and Dolly Parton, and she also loved the music of Elvis, moved by the tragedy of his short life. Later, in a ballad "Tupelo's Too Far," she recounted the sad underside of Presley's fame.

I never dreamed I would be a king, much less a star
I never knew that what I loved could also break my heart
I always thought if I just sang, everything would be all right
I don't know what went wrong, but I'm lonesome tonight

In her formative years, Campbell thought a lot about southern culture, particularly during her time at Auburn University, when she studied history under Professor Wayne Flynt. A native Alabamian from a working class family, Flynt was an expert on race and class in the South, and Campbell was so inspired by his teaching that she thought for a while of pursuing a career in academia. After earning her Masters degree at Auburn, she began work on a Ph.D. at Vanderbilt, but the lure of music was simply too strong.

With the support of her husband, Ira Campbell, she left Vanderbilt and pursued a full-time career as a songwriter. In 1998, she released an album called "Visions of Plenty" and many of us encountered her music for the first time. I remember hearing the title cut on a trip through western North Carolina, but the lyrics transported me back home – back to the Alabama-Mississippi world of painted sunsets and cotton fields blooming in the rich delta soil. Campbell captured the beauty of this part of the South, and she did it with a helping of irony and sadness.

She began writing the song on a trip back to Sledge, the Mississippi town where she was raised, and at first the images on Highway 61 were fully as beautiful as she had remembered, the cotton turning gold in the October sun. Then she began to notice the billboards, the garish, intrusive advertisements for casinos, and the false and cruel allure of easy money.

A sign went up for Harrah's on Highway 61
Promising we'd all be winners soon
So every Friday evening I go and spin the wheel
Sometimes I win, most times I lose

In Campbell's hands, "Visions of Plenty" became a poignant story of innocence lost, of rural people losing faith in the system and pursuing the new American Dream – not of success on the other side of hard work, but rather the hope of getting rich quick, which all too often only made things worse. Listening to the lyrics delivered in Campbell's silky soprano, with only the barest hint of a twang, I thought of the words of her favorite southern author, the great Mississippian, Eudora Welty.

"One place understood well," Ms. Welty once declared, "helps us understand all places better."

That has certainly been Campbell's hope, and thus she has chosen to write what she knows. Over the course of her fourteen albums, none of them hits, but all of them consistently praised by the critics, she has written about faith and family and civil rights, about the land and the people who struggle to make a living from it, and about southern literature and music. One of her best-known songs, "Crazy in Alabama," took its title from a

Mark Childress novel. Appearing first on her "Visions of Plenty" CD, with harmony vocals from Emmylou Harris, the song looks back on the turbulent civil rights years from the vantage point of a child. But over the course of Campbell's body of work, with its occasional dives into the South's murky waters, it is also clear that hers is a region she still loves.

Her song, "Look Away," inspired by a Eudora Welty interview on public television, makes the case, as Welty did, that even the antebellum South with its terrible, indefensible stain of slavery, was a place that yearned for culture and beauty. And thus the tainted history is double-edged.

It's a long and slow surrender, retreating from the past
It's important to remember to fly the flag half-mast

"There's a lot of 'Alabama' in my music," says Campbell, "a lot of things southern. I have spent my whole life in the fertile crescent of the South. I was born in New Orleans. My earliest memories are of the Mississippi Delta, and I've spent the majority of my life in Nashville. I also went to college in Alabama and spent some time as a songwriter there, and all these things are a part of who I am."

Will Kimbrough, a gifted songwriter from Mobile (he has written eight songs for Jimmy Buffett), has worked with Campbell on several of her albums. He says she's in a category of her own. "Kate is the consummate story-teller," Kimbrough maintains, "the consummate story-song writer. She's teaching history through her songs, which leaves her under the radar when it comes to show business, but very much on the radar in schools and universities and libraries – places where people are seeking greater substance. There really is nobody else like her."

That is certainly true as far as it goes, but among the ranks of Alabama songwriters, particularly the women, there are other artists who aim as high and understand the literature of the craft – the history and roots and higher calling of a song.

First and last, there is Emmylou Harris.

Boulder to Birmingham

One of my favorite country music memories is of Emmylou Harris at the Ryman Auditorium. This would have been around 1990 and the building had been standing empty for a while. In 1974, the Grand Ole Opry had moved from the Ryman to its slick new quarters at Opryland, an amusement park on what was then the outskirts of Nashville. Emmylou, among other artists, hated the silence at the dusty old shrine and was determined to do what she could to end it – to breathe new life into this most storied country music venue.

"I wanted to feel the hillbilly dust," she explained.

As her initial contribution to the Ryman's resurrection, she secured permission to cut a live album there. She was a little awestruck, she later explained, for Hank Williams had stood on that same stage, and Roy Acuff and Bill Monroe, and it was an eerie feeling as she gazed through the lights at the stained-glass windows and the benches that still resembled old pews. She surprised the audience that night with her choice of songs. One was "Lodi" from Credence Clearwater Revival, and there were back-to-back ballads from Stephen Foster and Bruce Springsteen, and then a song, both familiar and forgotten, by a little-known writer from Mobile.

Dick Holler had written "Abraham, Martin and John" as his personal response to the murder of Robert Kennedy. Before that summer of 1968, his biggest success had been a novelty number called "Snoopy vs. the Red Baron." Now, however, nothing seemed funny, and Holler did his best to capture the tragedy and loss of those times. He wrote his tribute, part anthem, part lament, for the martyrs to decency in American life – Abraham Lincoln, the Brothers Kennedy, and Martin Luther King.

For me, it was an unforgettable moment when Emmylou sang it on the stage of the Ryman. As a student of music, as well as a performer, she understood the role of songs during the turbulence of the civil rights years. It was said that Dr. King, in those dark days after the bombing of his home in Montgomery, would sometimes sit for hours in his office, listening to the old Negro hymn, "A Balm in Gilead." Mahalia Jackson's version, especially, provided the music to sooth his soul.

There were also, of course, the anthems sung by marchers in the streets, including the most famous of all, "We Shall Overcome," recorded by Joan Baez in Alabama. In 1963, Baez came to Miles College, an African-American school on the outskirts of Birmingham, and her live rendition of "We Shall Overcome" became a cornerstone of her album, "Joan Baez in Concert – Part 2." It was hard to imagine that only five years later, Dick Holler would be driven by the death of Robert Kennedy to write "Abraham, Martin and John" – his lyrics an epitaph for the times.

Didn't they try to find some good for you and me?

You could tell by the way she sang the words that Emmylou understood the fuller meaning of the song, the context in which it was written, and she wanted her audience to understand it as well. That had always been her gift, her deeper understanding of the purpose of music. From the time she left her home in Birmingham to pursue her career as a recording artist, she knew that music was the literature of the people. She may not have put it that way at first, but the realization was there in her instincts, and soon enough she met Gram Parsons. He came to hear her one night in 1971 when she was playing at a bar in Washington, D.C., a little singles club called Clyde's. She said there were maybe three people in the place when this famous rock 'n' roller stepped through the door, this refugee from Harvard and Waycross, Georgia, who had sung with the Byrds and the Flying Burrito Brothers, and had decided now to cut a country record.

He was looking for a girl to sing some harmonies, and during a break in Emmylou's set they headed off to the basement of Clyde's. They began working up songs, sitting there together on the kegs of beer, and there was something so lovely about the harmonies that they soon made a couple of albums together. Emmylou said her life was never the same. She began hearing music in a way she had never heard it before, and grew to love Gram Parsons as an artist and friend. When he died in 1973, apparently from the effects of too many drugs, it was one of the great devastations of her life, and she wrote "Boulder to Birmingham" in his memory, one of the finest love songs of her career.

> I would rock my soul in the bosom of Abraham
> I would hold my life in his saving grace
> I would walk all the way from Boulder to Birmingham
> If I thought I could see, I could see your face

"I'm always drawn to the lyrics first," she said years later, speaking in general about good country songs. "People know how hard life is. They need music that will give words and expression to the feelings they have. That's what country music is about. It has to be more than entertainment or escape."

For more than twenty years in a career that progressed "one song at a time," Harris was known for her ability to sing other people's songs. Her 1975 solo album, "Pieces of the Sky," featured a song from Paul McCartney and another from the Louvin Brothers, a renowned country band from Alabama. That was how it generally went until probably sometime in the 1990s when she set out to write more songs of her own. A breakthrough came with "Red Dirt Girl," a Grammy-winning album in 2001. The title cut, written by Emmylou, is a story song about innocence lost, set in the state where she was born.

> *Sittin on the front porch cooling in the shade*
> *Singin every song the radio played*
> *Waitin for the Alabama sun to go down*
> *Two red dirt girls in a red dirt town*

Emmylou would be the first to tell you – in fact, she's written about it in song – that her life has had more ups than downs: friends and lovers and husbands and music, all in the course of a brilliant career. And yet there's a sorrow that haunts her songs. It may be the generic preoccupation of country music, or it may be something more personal than that, some more intimate experience with loss. Certainly, that's the case with Allison Moorer, another of Alabama's finest songwriters, who burst upon the scene with an Oscar nomination.

The year was 1998, and Moorer's song, "A Soft Place to Fall," was featured in Robert Redford's "The Horse Whisperer." Moorer sang it herself in one of the movie's pivotal scenes, and sang it again at the Academy Awards. It was heady stuff for a girl of twenty-six who was born in Mobile and had graduated only five years before from the University of South Alabama. But as Redford himself was quick to note, it was a beautiful song – a wistful ballad about a young woman seeking temporary comfort in the bed of a lover with whom she has parted.

> *Looking out your window at the dawn*
> *Baby, when you wake up I'll be gone*
> *You're the one who taught me, after all*

How to find a soft place to fall

I thought when I heard it the first time in the movie, and again when they played it on the radio, that it was a song that flirted with Hank Williams territory – a country ballad that was almost perfect, both in the writing and in the delivery. The sadness was enough to break your heart, that palpable sense of longing and loss, and I remember wondering where it came from. What was the source of such feeling and depth?

I was not prepared for the answer, which emerged in the lyrics of another of Moorer's songs. On her second album, "The Hardest Part," there is a track called "Cold, Cold Earth," which ends with these lines.

Now they are lying in the cold, cold earth
Such a sad, sad story, such a sad, sad world

The song, which would sound like an old-fashioned folk ballad if not for the haunting cello in the background, tells the story of a murder-suicide: a drunken husband, driven mad with grief, kills his wife, who is determined to leave him, and then kills himself. The song is remarkable for its bravery, for the story is true. It happened in Moorer's family when she was thirteen, and her sister, Shelby Lynne, also an Americana singer, was seventeen, and they were living outside of Mobile. In her song Moorer performs, once again, the ancient alchemy of music, taking a moment so full of pain and turning it inexplicably into beauty. Part of the transformation was poetry, part the tender progression of the chords. But the song served notice that Moorer's motive was art, not top-forty stardom.

Over the course of eight studio albums she has written songs about addiction, broken hearts, and a loss of faith. And even her songs about happier times, including "Easy in the Summertime," from her 2010 album "Crows," seem to be layered with wistfulness and loss.

Swinging on the barnyard gate

It don't get dark till after eight
Run inside a kiss and hug
Wrapped up in my mama's love

"I think the thing about sad songs, really about art in general," Moorer says, "is that people are looking to connect with each other. That's why we make art. I just think that to do the job successfully, you have to find the common denominator, not the lowest common denominator, but that kind of shared experience where you take the personal and make it general."

In the end, she says, this is the literature of music.

Good Ole Boys Like Me

Pamela Jackson, one of the many Alabama songwriters now living in Nashville, came to the city expecting great things. "I had stars in my eyes," she admits. And why not? She was, and is, a good-looking woman who sings well and writes even better, and it never occurred to her that after thirteen years she would still be working at Brown's Diner, selling the finest hamburgers in town.

But she's also still writing songs, having taken her place within the ranks of writers who do it for love and not money or fame. Mostly, she says, she wouldn't change a thing – especially not after meeting Davis Raines. The two of them, fellow Alabamians, started writing together a few years back, meeting regularly once or twice a week, after she made the permanent move to Nashville. This was 1999, and since that time they have co-written maybe seventy-five songs, including in 2004, their own mini-classic, "Going to Montgomery." For Raines it became a signature song – the title cut of his third CD – confronting a time-honored theme in the South: the ambivalence that many of us feel about a place we love.

Rock me in the cradle
Where the moss hangs off the trees

Where it's hard and hot and hateful
Where it's soft and cool and sweet

Pamela had brought him the first two verses, and two lines into it Davis knew he was hooked: I'm going to Montgomery to march with Martin Luther King. I'm gonna shake these demons from me when I hear Hank Senior sing. He pondered the lines for a moment then suggested: "What if we make it 'walk' instead of 'march?'" It would set the song in a less specific time, and so they began to go through it that way, word by word, line by line, changing some things, leaving others, and adding enough to fill out the song. That is how they have always worked, like craftsmen building a chair or guitar, but knowing their raw materials are the heart and, sometimes, the raw underside of human emotion.

Davis, especially, has seen his share of that. He was born in Lee County, Alabama, where his father died when he was seven and his mother moved the family to a part of the state where the pulpwood forests give way to cotton. His stepfather, he says, was a "big rough son of a bitch," a prison guard who didn't waste a lot of time on sentiment. Somehow, it seemed a natural thing for Davis to follow his stepfather's path, and after four years at Auburn University Montgomery, where he earned a degree in criminal justice, he, too, went to work in Alabama's prisons.

Soon he was running a death row unit and life didn't get any harder than that. He came to know the inmates well, knew the heinous things they had done, but understood also that they were human beings. "I don't know that I was ever for capital punishment," he says. "I don't know what gives us the right to say who lives and who dies. And they had the electric chair back then. They had to hit John Louis Evans three times before pronouncing him dead."

Raines left the prison system in 1991 after a dispute with his warden, and following a year in graduate school, studying the

Romantic poets, he set about becoming a songwriter. He was fascinated by the Romantics – how Byron's anti-hero motif was there in the music of Waylon Jennings – and he saw immediately how the poets' method of composition could apply to writing songs. Somehow it left him feeling better, more at ease with his choice – so rash and unexpected on its face – to leave his "real job" and redefine himself as an artist.

He moved to Nashville in 1993, thirty-five years old with music in his heart. Inevitably, however, there were memories he couldn't shake – memories that continued to shape his songs. There was, for example, an inmate by the name of Willie Gaskey, whose job once a week was slaughtering pigs at the prison abattoir. It fell to Davis to oversee this work, to immerse himself in the blood and stench and the ear-splitting squeals on the killing floor. For his album, "Going to Montgomery," released in 2007, a long time after that work was behind him, Raines wrote a song called "Slaughterhouse." It was not specifically the story of Willie Gaskey, not of a prisoner doing what he was told, but rather of a man who has to have a job and is doing what he must to survive.

It ain't no sin to work and still be poor
But when you're doing this, friend, I ain't so sure

It was a song in the tradition of great country ballads about people on the margins – songs like Merle Haggard's "Hungry Eyes," telling the story of the migrant labor camps of California, or Tom T. Hall's "Mama, Bake a Pie," about a wounded soldier coming home from the war, or The Pirates of the Mississippi's "Feed Jake," a song with deep Alabama roots. In "Feed Jake," written by Alabama native Danny Mayo and sung by fellow Alabamian Bill McCorvey, the narrator of the song weaves the story of a guy and his dog with a message of tolerance for people on the edge – hookers and winos, a man who may be gay – all of it delivered in a gentle and reassuring baritone.

What we are and what we ain't

What we can and what we can't
Does it really matter?

Not long ago, I was talking to Raines about these songs, his own and those of other songwriters, and I asked how he came by his powers of empathy. It was one of those reporter's questions that's a little too direct, like something out of Barbara Walters' playbook, offending the subject's inclination to modesty. Raines, however, took it more or less in stride, though he thought for a minute before he replied.

"Anything that's good about me," he finally declared, "I got from my mama."

Whatever the source, his empathy interwoven with his craftsmanship is the gift that ultimately sets him apart, perhaps, even among his most gifted peers. Jon Byrd, an Alabama songwriter recently labeled a "genius" by *Maverick* magazine in England, calls Raines "the greatest songwriter in Nashville." Which raises the question in some people's minds, why isn't he famous?

It's a question that Davis dismisses out of hand. "It's all about the songs," he says. "It has to be."

He admits, of course, that the lure of fame or fortune is out there, and occasionally one or the other will descend – sometimes even upon people who deserve it. Jimmy Buffett, who grew up in Mobile, has sold millions of records with his "Margaritaville" sound, but he also wrote "He Went to Paris" and "A Pirate Looks at Forty," two of the most lyrical songs in country music. Hank Williams Jr., en route to his "Rowdy Friends" persona, wrote "Montana Song," a love ballad with a touch of his famous father's vulnerability, rendered with even greater finesse. And Lionel Richie, the soul balladeer who grew up on the campus of Tuskegee University, hit the top ten on the country chart with "Deep River Woman," which he wrote himself and sang to the harmonies of the country group Alabama. And the songwriters keep coming. From Sonny James in northern Alabama to Jamey Johnson in Enterprise, from the Band Perry with their ties to Mobile, to Tammy Wynette whose family farm when she was a girl straddled the Alabama-Mississippi line, they have plumbed the inspirations of home.

As Davis Raines and Pamela Jackson put their final touches on "Going to Montgomery," he says they headed south in their minds until they came to the place on I-65 where they could see the first streams of Spanish moss.

"Willie Morris talks about the burden of memory," Davis explains. "The great majority of everything I write is fueled by memories of Alabama."

I've thought about why that might be the case, and it seems to me, not surprisingly, that part of the answer is found in a song. In 1980, "Good Ole Boys Like Me," performed and written by a pair of Texans (Don Williams and Bob McDill, respectively), reached number two on the country chart with imagery about growing up southern – memories of Uncle Remus and Thomas Wolfe, and "the smell of cape jasmine thru the window screen" – and then a final affirmation in the chorus:

I can still hear the soft southern winds in the live oak tree
And those Williams boys, they sure mean a lot to me
Hank and Tennessee

Alabama's greatest songwriter is thus forever linked in song to a literary giant, and the two of them to the memories that make us who we are. There is something substantial about that identity. As Davis Raines put it in "Going to Montgomery," the demons inside us don't stand a chance – at least in the moment – whenever we hear Hank Williams sing.

Down on Mobile Bay

The first time I heard Kathryn Scheldt sing it was Sunday morning in a little oak-shaded chapel in Mobile, the late autumn sun slanting through the windows, as she sang of hope and mercy and despair. There was a power in the lyrics that seemed inseparable from the strength of her voice – a rich contralto that was different from anything I had heard. I had grown up in this particular church, and knew it as a place where the soprano voices of the Sunday morning choir paid their homage to the music of the past. But now here was Kathryn singing by herself – singing, as it happened, in the weeks just after Hurricane Katrina, and wrapping the heartache we could see all around us in the sacred compassion that came with her faith.

We are calling, can you hear it?
We are broken, bones and spirit
Rain down, Mercy, help us bear it
Shower us with love
Mercy, send a dove

This was a song, I discovered, that she had written herself, along with lyricist Anne Kent Rush, and it reminded me of something that might have come out of Nashville – which, in a sense, it had. Scheldt and Rush, both of whom live on Mobile

Bay, had made the pilgrimage up I-65 to stir some interest in their songs, and Kathryn was ready to make her first record.

I knew she would find her footing in Nashville. While there's nothing wrong with singing in church, I could see and hear with that first song that Scheldt's more natural home was country music. Or more precisely that blend of folk and country and blues that now goes under the name Americana.

About that time in my own career as a writer, I had returned again to the subject of music. I was working on a story about Peter Cooper, a Nashville songwriter with family ties to Andalusia, Alabama. Cooper had written an epic song called "715," an Americana tribute to the other famous "Hank" from Lower Alabama, Baseball Hall of Famer Hank Aaron. In 1974, Aaron had broken Babe Ruth's home run record, and for his troubles, had taken more than his share of abuse.

It struck me as a brilliant idea to write about this in a country song.

Jim Crow smilin' while the sun beat down
On a sandlot field on the wrong side of town

In researching the song, Cooper had pored over newspaper files until he came upon a story from 1957 – Aaron's third year in the majors – about an Aaron home run winning the pennant for the Milwaukee Braves. Aaron, then 23, was named the league's Most Valuable Player, and the newspaper showed him in the arms of his teammates, celebrating their triumph, while below the fold there were reports of race riots in Little Rock, Arkansas. In "715," Cooper captured the moment this way:

He won the pennant for the Braves with a four-base knock
The same day they were rioting in Little Rock
Up in ole Milwaukee he was MVP
Back in Alabama he was still not free
Not free to drink a beer in the white folks' lounge
Not free to have a meal in Mobile downtown

As he was writing that verse, Cooper called a friend, a steel guitar player by the name of Lloyd Green, to ask about its authenticity. Cooper knew Green had grown up in Mobile and would have known the city in its Jim Crow era. And when Green said, yes, Cooper's verse had it right, Cooper asked him to play on the record.

The result is stunning – a country song, fully six and a half minutes long, about the stoic heroism of an African-American baseball player. Musically, it's built around Green's pedal steel and Cooper's easy-going tenor voice, but the power comes mostly from the story it tells – the "truth and beauty," as the songwriter put it, that Aaron and his bat turned loose on the world.

I remember talking about the song with Kathryn, and I think that may have been when she suggested – much to my astonishment and shock – that I, too, should write a country song. I remember saying that I didn't do rhymes, but she said she would help me with that part, and soon we were writing a few lyrics together.

We wrote one of our early songs with Peter Cooper. We called it "The Last Shrimp Boat," and it was a song about a village on the Alabama coast. Bayou La Batre is a place where people have struck an ancient bargain with the sea – an understanding forged over time that the rewards of a man or woman's work are roughly equal to the sweat. Now, however, that article of faith has fallen prey to hard times. In recent years, hurricanes have battered the northern Gulf Coast, but the people on the Bayou have gotten used to that. What they are not used to and can't control is the price of diesel fuel, and the exorbitant expense of cranking up their boats. Though the bounty of the sea is still out there – and though they "love it like a farmer loves digging in the dirt" – they have begun to wonder if their treasured way of life will survive.

As always, we wanted to give the broader story a face, and though there was sadness at the heart of the song, there was redemption also in the strength of the people. In 2011, "The Last Shrimp Boat" was chosen for the soundtrack of *In the Path of the Storms*, a documentary film about the Alabama coast, produced by the Alabama Center for Public Television. It was, I thought, an important milestone for Kathryn's career as an artist, helping to secure her place in Mobile's recent Americana stream – among artists such as Keith Glass, Eric Erdman, Wes Loper, and Beverly Jo Scott.

In 2009, Kathryn's *Southern Girl* CD won her international acclaim – including a rave review in Australia's leading country music magazine – and airplay on more than 30 stations in the United States. For the recording of *Southern Wind* in 2010, Kathryn signed with Lamon Records, a fifty-year-old Nashville label whose roster includes George Hamilton IV of the Grand Ole Opry and the Grammy-nominated Moody Brothers. The next CD, *One Good Reason*, also released by Lamon, resulted in Kathryn's first chart hit. In 2012, her single, "Almost Cheatin'," made the top ten on the country chart and the top five on the indie. Now comes *The Quilt*, the CD that accompanies this book, and the fourth that features our co-written songs.

The lyrics that follow represent a sampling, and as we gathered them to be published here, we found ourselves reflecting again on the legacy of Alabama music. Whether with stories or feelings or snippets of irony in a good ole song, these musical poets we've come to admire have confronted the complexities of the heart.

We are happy to have our chance to do the same.

Part II – The Songs

Reflections by Kathryn Scheldt

Lyrics by Kathryn Scheldt and Frye Gaillard

Stories

Stories form the fabric of our lives...the shapes and patterns...the colorful things we do with them and the threads that hold them together...the ways we spin the yarn. When my great aunt passed away she left my dad her quilts. By the time I got to visit him, all the quilts had been divided among my brothers and sisters but there was a bag full of quilt scraps that no one knew what to do with ...so to rescue them from the Goodwill I brought them back home. They were so brightly colored and the fabrics seemed magical to me. Turned out that a friend of mine was a quilter by trade, and I asked her to have a look, since I could make neither reason nor rhyme of how they might ever be put together. Sarah studied the pieces and figured out the puzzle...a surprise quilt in the making...sewn by six women whose own signatures were in the style of their stitches and whose fingers had bled tiny stains into the patches. When Sarah brought me the finished product to see, I was totally amazed...a stunning family heirloom was created...a connection with the past brought into the present and to be passed on into the future. This seemed to be a good beginning for a song. When Frye and I started writing it, we centered the story around the legendary Gee's Bend Quilters...the quilt becoming a symbol of women working together and making art out of everyday life. Rick Hirsh had backed me on a gig or two, and I felt a certain "simpatico" with him as well as a deep admiration for his work, both as a guitarist and as a composer/producer. I thought it would be natural to bring his lowdown, get down, sophisticated style to "The Quilt." Turns out Frye and Rick were in the same graduating class in high school, and from the first brainstorming lunch at the Dew Drop Inn to the songwriting and recording sessions at Studio H2O on Dog River, our own quilt was in the making.

If "The Quilt" is essentially a song about love, I think all songs are about love in some way …That's why there is no chapter in this book called "Love." But there are love songs that are epic in scope, and "Casey in Love" is one of those. I discovered the story behind the song when I attended a funeral in Whistler, just north of Mobile, and saw an historical marker out front of St. Bridget's Church saying Casey Jones, the famous railroad engineer, was baptized there. I had wanted to get Frye really interested in writing songs, and I figured the historical significance of Casey Jones might spark his interest, and it definitely did. As we began our research, the incredible story unfolded...seems that Casey got baptized the second time so he could marry a Catholic girl he had met in a nearby boarding house while working in Mobile. The story became more and more fascinating as we began to write...and the story needed to be told. And as far as we can tell, every word of "Casey in Love" is true.

Another story that needed to be told is "Mama's Lullaby." My dear friend and producer, Mike Severs, had bumped a couple of songs off the last CD and told me to dig deeper with my writing...he said "I know you've got more in there." I remember thinking, "Oh no…" But then the pieces began to come together. For several years, I had the distinct and difficult honor of being

44

my mother's caregiver as she slugged it out with Alzheimer's. Once at lunch during that time I was talking with my cousin Maggie about how some nursery rhymes and prayers scare children, and I told her how my mama had changed some lines of the "Now I Lay Me Down To Sleep" prayer when I told her it was giving me nightmares. Maggie said, " Oh Kath…you should write that into a song…" That night I wrote 'Mama's Lullaby." The song in its entirety kept coming to me all night long….I kept hearing it over and over.. I wanted to get out of bed and write it down but I was afraid I'd lose the moment …so I stayed with it… just listened and embodied what I was hearing. When dawn broke I started writing…the story unfolded and I never edited one word. I grabbed my guitar and sang the song into my laptop...and then I fell apart…the emotional response was so intense it took several days to pull out of it. "Mama's Lullaby" is a tribute to my mother. She is the one who taught me about love. My Mama, Casey, the Quilters…the heartbeat goes on and on as stories stoke the fires of our memories and keep lighting up the way ahead.

The Quilt

Kathryn Scheldt, Frye Gaillard, Rick Hirsch, Nancy Gaillard
For the Quilters of Gee's Bend

Winter falls hard on this Alabama farm
In this ole cabin trying to stay warm
Light's pretty dim from a kerosene lamp
But I gotta keep my family from the cold and damp

Sewing them scraps like I see in my mind
All my quilts… one of a kind
Ain't aiming for no work of art
But all them stitches …come from my heart

And the quilt still hangs in Babygirl's house
Sweet reminder of what it's all about
Gotta be strong, gotta carry on
Gotta keep the children safe and warm

Sippin' sweet tea and talking 'bout life
Johnny's out runnin' with ole Preacher's wife
Patterns and shapes telling the tales
Needles move fast, making their trails

Traveling for miles in them ole kitchen chairs
All of us got a story to share
Sewing for birthdays or saying goodbye
And times I just wipe the tears that I cry

And the quilt still hangs in Babygirl's house
Sweet reminder of what it's all about
Gotta be strong, gotta carry on
Gotta keep the children safe and warm

Yeah, the quilt still hangs in Babygirl's house
Sweet reminder of what it's all about
Gotta be strong, gotta carry on
Gotta keep the children safe and warm
Safe and warm

The Last Shrimp Boat

Kathryn Scheldt, Frye Gaillard, Peter Cooper

Love it like a farmer loves digging in the dirt
Working for the harvest no matter what it's worth
I don't mind a little bit of sweating now and then
Just working on the water with a few good men
There's my cousin Rodney and our new neighbor Tran
Pulling in as many of them shrimp as we can
'Cause the warm Gulf waters have got what we need
And we've got our share of hungry mouths to feed
Yeah, we've got our share of mouths to feed

And the last shrimp boat's sailing with the dawn
New hard time's been coming on
Don't matter how you work or how you slave
On summer days out fighting with them waves

Now my ole man, he don't know what to think
Lately he's been getting pretty bad to take a drink
And the kids most nights are out there doing drugs
Falling in deeper with the ways of the world
Me, I spend most mornings at the seafood shop
Cleaning up the floors with that ole ragged mop
Pulling that sweet crabmeat from a thousand jagged shells
Finding myself crying when the church rings her bells
Yeah, crying when the church rings her bells

And the last shrimp boat's sailing with the dawn
New hard times been coming on
Don't matter how you work or how you slave
On summer days out fighting with them waves

48

The priest at St. Margaret's gives his blessing to the fleet
Praying every Sunday we can find a way to eat
Praying for a way of living through the hurt
Praying like the farmer is praying for the dirt

It's costing us a fortune now to gas up that ole boat
In the dog days the hurricanes come roaring up the coast
Working with our backs bent, as hard as we can stand
Debt upon our shoulders more than cash that's in our hands

And now the last shrimp boat's sailing with the dawn
New hard times keep coming on
Still I love it like a farmer loves digging in the dirt
Working for the harvest, no matter what it's worth
Yeah, working for the harvest, and knowing what it's worth

Rufus and Hank

Kathryn Scheldt, Frye Gaillard

Made a funny pair down by the railroad track
Skinny white boy and his friend who was black
Rufus Payne made his living on the streets
Playing his music so he had enough to eat
Bent those strings on his ole guitar
Feeling the music from way down in his heart
Hanging by his side every day there was Hank
People in the town didn't know what to think

Some of those songs sounded like a prayer
Touching the souls of people who were there
Every time he sang about a deep purple sky
And being so lonesome he could cry

When the demons came and haunted Hank's nights
Even when he sang about seeing the light
Most folks seemed to know just what he meant
Like all of his words must've been heaven-sent
But he knew they came from the Alabama dirt
A place where people understood the hurt
Where music was the thing that helped to keep 'em sane
A lesson he'd learned from his man Rufus Payne

Some of his songs sounded like a prayer
Touching the souls of people who were there
Every time he sang about a deep purple sky
And being so lonesome he could cry

Yeah, two southern men,
With nothing left to lose

50

Playing their hearts out
Singing their blues
Learning from each other
Sharing the pain
Knowing that the music
Was all keepin' 'em sane

Somehow his songs sound just like a prayer
Touching the souls of people everywhere
Every time he sang about a crawfish pie
Or being so lonesome he could cry
Yeah, being so lonesome he could cry

The Gospel According to Will

Kathryn Scheldt, Frye Gaillard
For Will Campbell

At night in his cabin he sang country songs
Strumming his parables about right and wrong
He loved the one about a Tennessee whore
When her lover showed up one day at her door
How he dried her eyes and sang her a song
Said, "C'mon, sweet Anna, I'm taking you home"

If you're gonna love one, you gotta love 'em all
Those were the words when Will heard the call
He knew the story 'bout the courthouse square
Near a statue of a general way over there
And a day that filled good people with shame
For things they had done in God's holy name

So he preached his gospel according to Will
And every time life was moving in for the kill
He'd sing that song about a cross on a hill
And the sweet love of Jesus raining down still

He knew his neighbors were all working hard
Fighting the weather and the Tennessee sod
He didn't care much about the color of their skin
Or just what shape their religion was in
He just knew Jesus came and he died
So God and sinners could be reconciled

Said, "We left that garden in such a shameful state
But all was not lost and it's never too late
There's just one thing to do with that fall

Love as much as you can, that's all"

Will had a farm where everybody came
Hillbilly singers and drifters in the rain
Sinners and preachers and people in pain
Ole Will he treated 'em all just the same
Rich or poor, a man in a robe
He gave 'em a place to lay down their load

Yeah, here's the gospel of ole Brother Will
In a world that's looking for something that's real
Just an ole sad song about a cross on a hill
And the sweet love of Jesus raining down still
The sweet love of Jesus raining down still

Geronimo's Cage
Kathryn Scheldt, Frye Gaillard

Grandpa told the story
He passed it down the line
How the train came roaring from the west
Steaming in on time
And a big crowd at the station
Came to see with their own eyes
A cargo brought from far away
From a land of endless skies

Now, grandpa he was just a boy
Holding daddy's hand
His young mind wandering wild and free
In that distant land
He could almost see Geronimo
Still riding on that paint
But they had him now behind the bars
On the last car of that train

And people said they once ran free
Riding with the wind
But now those days were gone for good
Never coming back again

Geronimo had killed his share
That's what folks all said
But now he just looked tired and old
His eyes were almost dead
Far from his desert mountains
Where he rode just like a ghost
His prison waiting 'round the bend

On the Alabama coast

Geronimo lived out his days
Though his spirit had been killed
No more distant mountains
No rocks and rugged hills
Just his braves and memories
Of the blood that they had spilled
And he listened for the sound
Of that lonesome whippoorwill

Apaches trapped behind the walls
Tried to reason why
The land was flat, the air was thick
And pine trees blocked the sky
And Grandpa still remembers
The day he came of age
Didn't know why he cried that night
For a legend in a cage

And the people said they once ran free
Riding with the wind
But now those days were gone for good
Never coming back again

Now those days are gone for good
Never coming back again

Casey in Love

Kathryn Scheldt, Frye Gaillard

A boy from Kentucky, he was born feeling lucky
A lover of the rails and speed
But a blond-haired beauty in an old boarding house
Said, "Baby, I'm the one you need"
As the love light danced in her deep southern eyes
Something took him by sweet surprise
Yeah, the boy from Kentucky knew he was lucky
Under warm Tennessee skies

He loved the green rolling hills and the worn cotton fields
And the live oaks down by the Bay
Louisiana mornings and Mississippi nights
But none of them could make him stay
He was searching for his freedom, half wishing he was home
'Cause it's a long way to nowhere and sad to be alone
But the boy from Kentucky knew he was lucky
Under soft Tennessee skies

Ribbon of steel, big engine wheel
Cutting through the heart of the South
Wind in his hair, life without care
That's what he'd sing about
Lending a hand, an ear or a dime
Steady at the wheel gotta get her there on time
Searching for his freedom, half wishing he was home
'Cause it's a long way to nowhere and sad to be alone

In a little white church not far from the Bay
He got down on his knees in prayer
Breeze blowing soft 'neath the cedar tree shade

He was wishing that his Janie was there
He got baptized on that bright sunny day
He couldn't wait to hear what she would say
But the boy from Kentucky knew he was lucky
He married her straight away

Now Casey's a man with a wife and child
His blood doesn't run so wild
The moonlight danced in her deep southern eyes
Under dark Tennessee skies
Late in the spring, they were saying goodbye
Janie kissed her Casey with a tear in her eye
She knew her man had a job to do
She just said, "Baby I'll be waiting for you"

Ribbon of steel, big engine wheel
Cutting through the heart of the South
Wind in his hair, life without care
That's what he'd sing about
Lending a hand, an ear or a dime
Steady at the wheel, gotta get to her on time
Searching for his freedom, half wishing he was home
'Cause it's a long way to nowhere and sad to be alone

Casey had friends in the railroad yard
Black or white, they all worked hard
When the union came, it was one for all
And he listened when that whistle called
As the iron horse roared through the wounded land
Where the soldiers' blood ran deep in the sand
People in the towns where the hurt never healed
Found hope in the ribbon of steel

Heavy on the throttle, they were running behind
Trying hard to make up some time
Eighty miles an hour through that Mississippi night
When something just didn't look right
Sim saw it coming, Casey knew it looked too tough
Got her down to 40 but that wasn't enough
He blew his final whistle in that Mississippi swamp
And he told all his buddies to jump

Hand on his heart with the brakes in his hand
Casey knew that day he'd see the Promised land
But the boy from Kentucky knew he was lucky
Living the life of a railroad man.
The yards got quiet when the word came down
Ole Saunders made him famous, told his story all around
But the words of his song still cut like a knife
'Bout a man in love with a woman and his life

Ribbon of steel, big engine wheel
Cutting through the heart of the South
Wind in his hair, life without care
That's what he'd sing about
Lending a hand, an ear or a dime
Steady at the wheel, gotta get her there on time
Casey found that freedom. He finally made it home
Remember his story, he'll never be alone
Remember his story, he'll never be alone

So Easy

Kathryn Scheldt, Frye Gaillard

She remembers a smile when he heard the old songs
Telling the world not to do people wrong
And when he learned to play on his own
They sang with Dylan and Guy Carawan
They sang their harmonies with the Byrds
When Baez played they knew every word
And when they marched behind Dr. King
They believed when he said they could let freedom ring

Just waiting to live all the words they would sing
Yeah, waiting to live all the words they would sing
Life was so easy then
They were in love and it was way back when
They were in love and it was way back when

But then one morning he was saying goodbye
A smile on his face, but fear in his eye
And when his letters came from Da Nang
He said there were new songs now that he sang
He tried to tell her how it all seemed
The jungles burned and the children would scream
The sergeant's orders kept bringing him down
While far away in a Carolina town …

She was waiting for the love that couldn't be found
Yeah, waiting for the love that couldn't be found
Nothing was so easy then
She was in love and afraid it would end
She was in love and afraid it would end

Kept writing those letters to her friend far away
Hoping and praying he'd be coming home to stay
Living for those letters and waiting for the news
Playing his guitar and singing his blues
Yeah, playing his guitar and singing his blues

When he finally came home they roared through the town
The radio up and the windows rolled down
He was living hard in his deep purple haze
And most of his nights were worse than his days
He was doing his LSD and his H
But nothing could stop his terror or the ache
It broke her young heart when she had to move on
Hearing her story in that Dolly Parton song

Her new lovers came and then they would go
And all she could do was pray for his soul
Nothing was ever so easy again
They were in love, but it was way back when
They were in love, but it was way back when

Southern Girl

Kathryn Scheldt, Frye Gaillard

Well a southern girl came to the big city
She was not so young, but still kind of pretty
And she left her job and her family, too
She said, "I gotta tell it like it is as only I can do"

Well when she got to that crowded town
She felt so lonely when she looked around
She missed the sunshine of a summer's day
And the moon laying low down on Mobile Bay

She's walking the line
She's making a plan
She's paying the price
She's taking a stand
She's cutting the cost
She's footing the bill
She knows what she's worth
Both hands on the wheel

Then she met a man who came from Bermuda
Well he looked alright, though she'd seen cuter
But she got excited by the things he'd say
And his funny way of talking far from Mobile Bay

There's a new southern girl in the city
She's still kind of young, and so damn pretty
And she hears her Mama and her Daddy, too
Saying, "Baby, tell it like it is as only you can do"

She's walking the line

She's making a plan
She's paying the price
She's taking a stand
Eyes on the prize
She's closing a deal
She knows what she's worth
Both hands are on the wheel

Both hands on the wheel

Selma

Kathryn Scheldt, Frye Gaillard, Ennio Incerti

The children on the bridge
Can see a better life
They know the way to get there
Through the hard and bitter night
They are not afraid
Of the drifting gas
They believe with all their hearts
The dream is gonna last

Marching cross the river, singing as they go
Just trying to believe the truth that they've been told
They have dreams of justice and liberty for all
They believe that promise, they have heard the call

Give to me your tired
Yearning to breathe free
The lady in the harbor
So beautiful to see
But when they cross the border
In the dead of night
We pass laws to send them home
Sure that we are right

Marching for their freedom, marching for ours too
Marching for an angry land, not sure what to do
They have dreams of justice and liberty for all
They believe that promise, they have heard the call

The children on the bridge
Could see a better life

They knew the way to get there
Through the hard and bitter night
They were not afraid
Of the drifting gas
But now they sing a sadder truth
Of dreams that never last

Marching cross the river, singing as they go
Just trying to believe the truth that they've been told

Mama's Lullaby

Kathryn Scheldt
For Joan Young Tonelli

Mama tucked me in that night, she said "it's time to say our
prayers"
I said I didn't want to do it…that I was really scared
"What's God gonna do with my soul if I should die?"
She held me close and said, "now baby, there's no need to cry…

Just close your eyes and go to sleep
Pray to God your soul to keep
Guide you through the starry night
And wake you with the morning light"

And I remember one day I came crying home from school
Said I was never going back…I felt just like a fool
That note on my desk made me so mad that I could scream
It said "you're flatter than a board…a carpenter's dream"

Oh Mama, the boys they laugh at me 'cause I'm too tall and thin.
Nobody wants to dance with me. Where do I fit in?
She said, "Doll baby, I know how you feel, so dry those pretty
eyes

Growing up is hard sometimes, but soon you'll realize
That you are loved and you are beautiful
Because I say it's true…and I believe in you
So stand up tall … and don't be shy"
This was Mama's lullaby

Now life is good for me, I've settled down with my old man
The kids are off at college, but Mama keeps losing ground

Some days she barely knows my name but she when she takes my hand
With a touch only a mother knows, we both understand
... we both understand

So close your eyes and go to sleep
Pray to God your soul to keep
Guide you through the starry night
And wake you with the morning light
'Cause you are loved and you are beautiful
Because I say it's true...and I believe in you
So stand up tall ... and don't be shy
This is Mama's lullaby
My mama's lullaby

Feelings

*We are here for the sake of others...for the countless unknown
souls with whose fate we are connected by a bond of
sympathy....*

– Albert Einstein

This was my music mentor Aaron Shearer's favorite quote
and so often he reminded me that all the refining of one's craft
is for one purpose...to share. By that simple act we let each
other know that we are not alone. This chapter is a collection of
songs that express deep feelings. They say that art comes from
inspiration and I believe that's true...but sometimes for me it feels
more like desperation. It's like the voice of God is telling me to
pay attention and all I can do is listen and write down what I hear.
Sometimes these lyrical "spasms," as Frye and I have come
to call them, are so overwhelming they can wake me up in the
middle of the night. Once during a violent thunderstorm, a melody
and its words called out from some hidden place. I fumbled for
my bedside notebook and started writing. This became the song
"Every Shade of Blue." And then one evening at sunset I was
walking on the pier in my hometown of Fairhope, Alabama, and
noticed that my walking gait was in 3 / 4 time and I was walking

to a tune I was hearing for the first time. This experience became "Across the Wide Water."

The first song Frye and I ever wrote together, "Words Get in the Way," was also conceived on the Fairhope pier...I called Frye and asked him to give it a try...to see what the title meant to him. He pretty immediately called me back with what became the chorus and we were off to the races. I had gone to Frye earlier and asked him to look at some writing I had been hiding away in my journals to see if I should take it seriously or just burn all the boxes. He encouraged me to go public with what I was writing, which was coming from such an emotional place it scared me. But the more I continued to share it, the better I felt. And the cool thing about writing with Frye is that he can get right into my psyche and share or even understand where I'm coming from. When we write together it feels like we are one mind.

Even without hearing the music, I hope you find something in these songs that strikes a chord or rings a bell...or maybe makes you feel something new.

Every Shade of Blue

Kathryn Scheldt, Frye Gaillard

So where it's coming from, I wonder
In the stillness of the night
And there just like a crash of thunder
I'm in your arms so tight
Bare, I surrender
Believe I'm holding you
And I'm counting
Every shade of blue

Like a prayer I cry aloud
With the voices of the wind
Dare let the dream take over
And then I'm lost again
Full of hope and wonder
I'm praying that it's true
And I'm counting
Every shade of blue

In a world of black and white
A world of day or night
In a world of right or wrong
I still dream a lover's song

When the night storm dies
With traces of the dawn
Seabird drifts through hazy skies
And then you're gone
Here, I surrender
What my heart knows is true
And I'm counting

Every shade of blue

Yeah, I'm counting every shade of blue

Words Get in the Way

Kathryn Scheldt, Frye Gaillard

Caught between the earth and sky
Caught up in a dream
Lost between the day and night
Can this be what it seems?
'Cause every time I think of you
I don't know if it's true
I'll touch you with my fingertips
Can you read me with your lips?

Alone with just a feeling
The words like shadows fall
But every time I see you
Can't find the words at all

So many nights without you
Such a heavy price to pay
It's a dark and lonesome feeling
When words get in the way

What if we could find ourselves
Beyond the world of time
Travel someplace far away
A place just yours and mine
What if we could make it real
Not just a lovers' dream
And jump in risky waters
Well, that's alright with me

So many nights without you
Such a heavy price to pay

It's a dark and lonesome feeling
When words get in the way

We can swim, we can sink, what a way to go
We can dance and take a chance, we can let it show

'Cause every time I see you
I don't know what to say
Just search my heart for explanations
And throw the words away

Throw the words away

Phoenix

Kathryn Scheldt, Frye Gaillard

I've been cheated and I've been burned
I've risen from the ashes of love
To take another turn
Like the phoenix from the flames
I've given all I've got
Only to give again

I've turned the other cheek
Turned myself around
Turned away
Turned it loose
Turned it upside down
Turned it on
Turned it off
Turned it inside out,
Baby, that's what love's about.

I've learned the hard way. I've learned it well
I've learned that living life in fear
Is living life in hell
I'm through with running
I'm through with games
If love is really all there is
We better fan the flames

And turn the other cheek
Turn ourselves around
Turn away
Turn it loose
Turn it upside down

Turn it on
Turn it off
Turn it inside out
That's what love's about....
Yeah, Baby, that's what love's about

Do It With Me

Kathryn Scheldt

You didn't do it for me
You didn't do it to me
I wasn't asking you to
But somehow you knew....
You did it with me

You didn't pass up the chance
To set our love free
You didn't think about you
But somehow you knew
You did it with me

You walked right through
The door of my heart
Baby I never knew
How good it could feel
Till I fell apart

Now every road that I'm on
Everything that I see
It's not about why
We don't have to try
You'll do it with me
Do it with me...do it with me...

Across the Wide Water
Kathryn Scheldt, Frye Gaillard

Across the wide water
Reaching out for the sky
They're touching each other
As the day says goodbye

And you had your reasons
For going away
Across the wide water
Said you'd come back some day

I waited that winter
Spring, summer and fall
Looked across the wide water
Hoping I'd hear your call

Wondering if you were seeing
The same silver moon
Reach across the wide water
To bring you home soon

With a heart that's as big as the sea and the sky
Still couldn't help thinking and wondering why
So I crossed the wide water, I just had to see
What was waiting beyond the horizon for me

Across the wide water
I found other loves
As the breeze rustled gently
Through the boughs up above

But the wide waters called
And carried me home
Where the moon's shining softly
And I'm waiting alone

Where the moon's shining softly
And I'm waiting alone

Fairhope

Kathryn Scheldt, Rick Hirsch, Frye Gaillard

Some folks paint a picture where the water shines like gold
Some catch that moment in a photograph
There's a place that lives in a better time
Getting better like vintage wine
Some folks come from all around
Come to stay in my hometown
And it ain't hard to find a happy smile

Me, I'm just singing this ole song
The clock says 2 a.m. and I'm gone
Riding cross those railroad tracks
Ain't no way I'm looking back
Fairhope waits for me
I'm going home

Spainish moss is hanging from a live oak tree
Cicadas singing their harmony
There's a place that moves at a different pace
Moves with such a peaceful grace
Listen to their siren song
Telling you to come on down
And drop your sails and rest for a while

Me, I'm just singing this ole song
The clock says 2 a.m. and I'm gone
Riding cross those railroad tracks
Ain't no way I'm looking back
Fairhope waits for me
I'm going home

Me, I'm just singing this ole song
The clock says 3 a.m. and I'm gone
Riding cross those railroad tracks
Ain't no way I'm looking back
Fairhope waits for me
I'm going home

Fairhope waits for me
I'm going home

Pretend

Kathryn Scheldt

Yeah, Baby, it's been a long time
Since I was yours
And you were mine
Seems like now all we do is pretend
That we're not lovers
We're just good friends
It's a game
This lie that we're living
Such a shame
Why don't we just give in?

It would be so good
It would be so right
If we could make it happen
For just one night
Looks like we'll never be free
'Cause she's got you
And he's got me

Yeah , Baby, I know that there's a way
To make it happen
For just one day
I ask myself over and over again
But I always come back
To where I begin
It's alright
I know I can make it
Take my heart
I won't let you break it

It would be so good
It would be so fine
If we could make it happen
Just one more time
So meet me halfway
Let's pretend that it's true
That you've got me
And I've got you
That you've got me, and I got you

Naturally
Kathryn Scheldt, Rick Hirsch

Look at me
Do you see
Something happens
Naturally
It's impossible to say
If loving leads the way
But baby
It's the only way for me

Show me how
Tell me when
I can learn
To love again
It's impossible to know
Where the road we're on will go
But on the way
It's good to have a friend

They tell us that the journey is always worth the climb
They tell us that on the way we'll fall
What's gonna happen if halfway to the top
You hear love call?

Look at me
Do you see
Something happens
Naturally

I'm climbing
Then I fall

But it don't scare me at all
'Cause when you bring me to my knees
It comes so naturally

What's it matter?
Maybe not at all
What's it matter … maybe not at all

Southern Wind

Kathryn Scheldt, Frye Gaillard

Southern wind
Steady and strong
Carries my dreams
All the night long
Smell of your hair
Taste of your skin
Carried away
On a soft southern wind

The sound of a songbird
Drifting from the past
Such a sweet reminder
The night can never last

Southern wind
Steady and strong
Carries my hopes
All the day long
Seeing you here
Then gone again
Carried away
On a soft southern wind

The time of white blossoms
In her darkest hour
Feeling impossible
What's happened to that flower?

Southern wind
Steady and strong

My hopes and dreams
Moving along
I can't come back
This way again
So carry me on
On a soft southern wind

Carry me on…
Soft southern wind

Georgiana

Kathryn Scheldt, Frye Gaillard, Tom Morley

There's an old railroad track through the heart of my town
But the Hummingbird train, she never slows down
And an old lonesome sound as I close the door
Says I can't come back home anymore

Looks like a ghost out walking the street
Like an old blues singer I never did meet
Like a sweet gospel tune I hear in my mind
Like the peace I'm hoping to find

Ask me why, I don't know
But I just have to go
Where I've never been before
Every time I look back
My dreams turn to black
Saying I can't go back home anymore

Wild chestnut horse in the meadow at dawn
Free as the robin when she knows spring is born
Pages may fade and time slip away
While the music moves me along

Ask me why, I don't know
But I just have to go
Where I've never been before
Every time I look back
My dreams turn to black
Saying I can't go back home anymore
And I can't go back home
Anymore

Good Ole Songs

When asked about the key to his craft, the great Nashville songwriter Vince Matthews said, "Man, you gotta live it." I think that's true. It is, for sure, the key to writing what I would call a "good ole song." It's the kind of song that may not attempt to be profound, but it does come out of real life...from everyday encounters or experiences that seem to have such a communality – or a uniqueness – that they are worth sharing. This is the case with "Desperate Diva." Last year I sang an evening gig in Atlanta where I was staying with my sister and her family. The next morning, in a pre-coffee stupor, I staggered into the kitchen where my brother-in-law Tom was quietly having his breakfast, and I proclaimed:

> *"Desperate Diva's got a heavy load*
> *early this morning she's hitting the road*
> *worked all her life just to get this far*
> *selling CD's from the trunk of her car..."*

Tom just looked at me over his cereal and morning paper and replied, "You're weird." I told Frye that story and we started writing the rest of it, totally inspired by events of the road trip, and then we sent it off to my producer who encouraged us further. It's a song about giving your best...not getting discouraged by life…knowing you can move through the moments of desperation and stay your course.

Once before singing a song of mine, "Pretend," I mentioned that there are a lot of country songs about cheatin' but that this was my song about almost cheatin'. After the show, Frye's wife, Nancy, came up to us and said, "Y'all should write a song called Almost Cheatin'!" Frye took her comment to heart and started writing. When he sent me the first draft I got pretty excited about it…I knew we were hitting the double standard pretty head on in this one. It became our first single from "One Good Reason" and our first song to make it to the top ten, which just proved to us that we were on to something. I played the song for Shelly, my friend and household helper, and after listening through the second verse – and the line that says, "When a woman does it they call it a sin" – she looked at me and said, "Ain't it the truth." Now that's a good ole song.

Southerners love food and we have written a couple of good ole songs about that, including "Barbeque Girl," which just talks about the irresistible impulses inspired by barbeque. My dad, who made me the barbeque girl that I am, even penned a line in this song… "take it easy…cook it low and slow…" So help yourself and enjoy!

A Lowdown Dirty Shame

Kathryn Scheldt, Frye Gaillard
For Albert Murray

Ole man hears it in his mind
Sweet blue notes all one of a kind
Ain't nobody 'round here to blame
Life's just a lowdown, dirty shame

North star shining in a midnight sky
Sound of a freight train rattling by
Slave and free man all the same
Life's just a lowdown dirty shame

Star, it'll lead you
Where you need to go
Blues, they'll teach you
What you need to know
Stars don't mind
If you're red, white or black
Got an arm full of freight train
Never looking back

Ole man hears it in his mind
Sweet blue notes all taking their time
Ain't nobody 'round here to blame
Life's just a lowdown dirty shame
Life's just a lowdown dirty shame

Desperate Diva

Kathryn Scheldt, Frye Gaillard

People always said she was weird
Singing 'bout all the things that she feared
Lovin' and losin' and settlin' down
She's heading out for another town
Desperate diva's got a heavy load
Early this morning she's hitting the road
Worked all her life just to get this far
Selling CD's from the trunk of her car

Tonight Mississippi… tomorrow Tennessee
She's only going where she wants to be
Some of those men might have treated her wrong
But that's alright, it made a good song
Yeah, that's alright… it made a good song

She was singing in the lounge at the Holiday Inn
She saw this guy come walking in
Bought her a drink from the Holiday bar
Said "come on let's make you a star"
Next thing you knew the wedding was planned
And a big record contract there in her hand
But the night before signing he left her in tears
With ten chafing dishes and a bottle of beer

Tonight Mississippi… tomorrow Tennessee
She's only going where she wants to be
Some of those men might have treated her wrong
But that's alright, it made a good song
Yeah, that's alright… it made a good song

Sees a homeless man on the street
Holding a sign about something to eat
Gave him a smile and a couple of tens
Back in the car on the road again
Says to herself, "now don't you see
With a little less luck that could have been me
Never been down to my last dime
Only been lonely some of the time"

Tonight Mississippi… tomorrow Tennessee
She's only going where she wants to be
Some of those men might have treated her wrong
But that's alright, it made a good song
Yeah, that's alright… it made a good song

Desperate diva's got a heavy load
Early this morning she's hitting the road
Worked all her life just to get this far
Selling CD's from the trunk of her car…

Almost Cheatin'

Kathryn Scheldt, Frye Gaillard, Nancy Gaillard

Baby I love you, I know it's still true
Don't know why I do what I do
Same old obsession keeps bringing me down
Sad song playing on the wrong side of town

The neon calls and I'm looking good
Keep on hoping I'll do what I should
But the music plays, and I leave it to fate
One of these nights it'll be too late

Almost cheatin'... hadn't made it yet
Night of sweet lovin' … hard to forget
Out there roaming … looking around
While a sad song keeps playing on the wrong side of town

They say a woman shouldn't do what I do
Oughta be back at home loving you
They say it's not the same for a man
When a woman does it, they call it a sin, yeah

Almost cheatin'... hadn't made it yet
Night of sweet lovin' ... so hard to forget
Out here roaming... looking around
While a sad song keeps playing on the wrong side of town

Yeah, a sad song keeps on playing on the wrong side of town

Drinkin' About You

Kathryn Scheldt, Frye Gaillard

You went away and left me
By myself and all alone
And all I've got to think about
Is, baby, now you're gone
You left me with a pickup truck
And a bottle of Jim Beam
And I'd rather drink than think about
This ole lonesome scene

I don't do much thinking
All it does is make me blue
Drinkin'? Yeah, I'm drinkin'
I'm drinkin' long and hard about you

Now you're out there running
With that pretty dark-eyed girl
Left me here to think about
This crazy, mixed up world
I know I'm not the only one
Who's living without a hope
But I'd rather drink than think about
The end of this ole rope

So I don't do much thinking
All it does is make me blue
Drinkin'? Yeah, I'm drinkin'
I'm drinkin' long and hard about you

I know some folks are hungry
And down to their last dime

I know I'm not the only one
Who's been left behind
But that don't seem to help too much
Don't make it all less true
So I'm out here filling up a glass
And I'll drink this round for you

I don't do much thinking
All it does is make me blue
Drinkin'? Yeah, I'm drinkin'
I'm drinkin' long and hard about you

Drinkin'? Yeah, I'm drinkin'
I'm drinkin' long and hard about you

Stop Stoppin'

Kathryn Scheldt

Drove all the way from Mobile to Memphis
Just lookin' for a minute of your time
I'm keepin' cool. I'm nobody's fool
But I think it's time to lay it on the line
All these places keep leaving their traces
Of something I can't get off my mind
Can't erase it. Keep trying to chase it
So I guess I better lay it on the line

Stop stoppin' what you started
Start doin' what you said
Don't leave with just a promise
Gotta get you out my head
Are you trying to drive me crazy?
Don't you think it's kind of rude?
I'm getting tired of 'maybe'
Don't leave me with my heart come un-glued

There's a fine line between right and wrong
And the right time seems to never come
So stop telling me what you're gonna do
'Cause what's right for me's always wrong for you

Seems like we're going nowhere fast
Don't you think it's kind of rude?
So stop stoppin' what you started
Don't leave me with my heart come un-glued

My heart come un-glued
Heart come un-glued

Wishes

Kathryn Scheldt, Frye Gaillard

If only the leopard could change her spots
I would never need to be something I am not
If my wishes were granted by the distant star
I'd never be without your love no matter where you are

If I had a penny for all of my thoughts
I'd lock all that money up in a Swiss vault
And I would hold you right here by my side
If wishes were horses ... beggars would ride

The way you loved me left me wanting more
Praying for your footsteps outside my back door
But wishes won't keep me warm in the night
Knowing what's wrong still don't make it right

If I had a penny for all of my thoughts
I'd lock all that money up in a Swiss vault
And I would hold you right here by my side
If wishes were horses ... beggars would ride

If wishes were horses, then beggars too would ride

Barbeque Girl

Kathryn Scheldt, Frye Gaillard, Richard Scheldt, Sr.

Well she's a barbeque girl, she loves a good man
They're trying to hit every joint that they can
He takes her to Cotten's and the ole Rib Shack
The Land of Dreams and the Pit out back
Up in Memphis there's the place on Beale
The brisket in Austin and a dive in Mobile

There's a little woodshack on the Selma highway
That people in a hurry pass by every day
Bear Bryant's picture hanging crooked on the wall
And Martin Luther King staring down from the hall
Barbeque beans leave you wanting more
And Brunswick stew's the kind to die for

That barbeque girl, she loves 'em all
Can't help herself when the blue smoke calls
Yeah, can't seem to help herself at all
No, can't seem to help herself at all

She remembers when summer vacation came 'round
She and her Daddy'd take a trip downtown
They'd fill up the trunk, not with bottles of brew
But with jugs of that sauce for making barbeque
Waiting for the coals to shimmer just so
Pecan wood smoking and ready to go

When God's gets hungry, Lucille's on the phone
He's wanting something juicy and falling off the bone
Her recipe's from heaven—it's tried and it's true
It's sure to make a believer out of you

It don't matter if you're white or you're black
Just start something smoking when we step out back

That barbeque girl, she loves it all
Can't help herself when that blue smoke calls
Yeah, can't seem to help herself at all
No, can't seem to help herself at all

From the mountains down to the Louisiana coast
She remembers those days with her Daddy the most
But she's riding now with another good man
Stopping at every little barbeque stand
Don't matter if it's hog meat, gator or goat
Can't help herself when she smells that smoke

That barbeque girl, she loves it all
Can't help herself when that blue smoke calls
Yeah, can't seem to help herself at all
No, can't seem to help herself at all

So help yourself when you feel it call
Help yourself to a little of it all
Smell it, taste it, turn it, baste it
That's the way to go
Take it easy
Cook it low and slow
Take it easy
Cook it low and slow

Life in a Hurry
Kathryn Scheldt, Frye Gaillard

Old man plowing a long, straight row
Him and his mule both taking it slow
Little boy playing without a care
Skipping by on his way to nowhere
Old man smiles, says "boy, don'tcha worry
You'll get there even if you don't hurry"

Young man talking on a Blackberry phone
Cursing traffic and wishing he was gone
Boy on a skateboard pushing along
iPod blasting a rock 'n' roll song
Woman in a cab, face full of worry
Says, "we'll never get there if we don't hurry"

Living our lives at breakneck speed
Forgetting about everything we need
Blackberry blossom on a summer day
A hand to hold and
A place to stay
Sunset making a path for the stars
God and Jesus
And ending the wars
But most of all, a chance to slow down
And reach for the beauty
We see all around

Pretty woman wanting answers right away
Is it love, is he gonna stay?
Man at dinner, playing it cool
A little action's the modern rule

She smiles and says, "hey, don't you worry
We'll get there if we don't hurry"

Lying softly when the shadows fall
Searching for a way to say it all
But taking the time to say it right
Even if it takes all night
He says, "baby don't you worry
Love is real, no need to hurry"

Learning how to take our time
Trying to find our rhythm and rhyme
Breezes blowing on a summer day
A hand to hold and a place to stay
Sunset making a path for the stars
God and Jesus
And ending the wars
But most of all, a chance to slow down
And reach for the beauty
We see all around

Baby girl saying her prayers at night
Mama and Daddy tuck her in real tight
Kitty cat purring, cuddling up real close
Sweet dreams coming in a heavy dose
Her little eyes are tired and blurry
She's fast asleep without a worry

Taking time out from the long day's troubles
Soaking her bones in a bath full of bubbles
Mama tells Daddy her feet are hurting
She's pulling his leg. He knows she's just flirting
Taking the time to do it right

It's okay, we've got all night

Just as long as we're alive
Remember time is on our side
Fields of clover on a summer day
A hand to hold, a place to stay
Moonlight making a path for the stars
God and Jesus
And ending the wars
But most of all, a chance to slow down
And reach for the love
We see all around

A Perfect World

Kathryn Scheldt, Frye Gaillard
For George Hamilton IV

In a perfect world
We'd always have enough
In a perfect world
Even when the times get rough

We can work it out
With music and justice for all
Allelu
Allelu

In God we trust
We're walking hand in hand
Working side by side
To build a promised land

Sing a song of truth
With music and justice for all
Allelu
Allelu

So come on, everybody
Gotta keep moving on
Gotta work with each other
And bear the heavy load
We can make it together
Heal our precious land
As we share in the dream
Every woman, child and man

In a perfect world
We all live as one
In God we trust
Our faith has kept us strong

Sing a song of truth
With music and justice for all
Allelu
Alleluia

LA Girl

Kathryn Scheldt, Frye Gaillard

I ain't rich, but I ain't poor
Sure ain't cheap, but I ain't pure
Looking for love as much as I can
Out there chasing just the right man

I'm an LA girl, an LA girl
Living my life on the edge of the world
Riding along on those dusty back roads
Fields of cotton, soft southern snow

I'm an LA girl, I don't give a damn
It's Lower Alabama where I'm taking my stand
They say I'm crazy for living down here
Putting it out there feeling no fear

I'm an LA girl, an LA girl
Living my life on the edge of the world
Riding along on those dusty back roads
Fields of cotton, soft southern snow

Hurricanes come and they fly away
An oil slick's drifting out on the bay
But this is my home and there ain't no way
I'll ever let 'em drive me away

'Cause I'm an LA girl, an LA girl
Living down here on the edge of the world
Riding along on those dusty back roads
Fields of cotton, soft southern snow

Yeah, I'm an LA girl, an LA girl
LA girl, sweet LA girl...

Contributors

Frye Gaillard, author and songwriter, is writer in residence at the University of South Alabama. A native of Mobile, he has written more than twenty books and has received the Clarence Cason Award for Non-Fiction, the Lillian Smith Book Award, and the Alabama Library Association Book of the Year recognition.

Kathryn Scheldt, author, singer and songwriter, is a resident of Fairhope and author of two guitar songbooks for Mel Bay Publications. Kathryn has played listening rooms all over the South, and has released six solo CDs to international acclaim. Her single, "Almost Cheatin'," from her "One Good Reason" CD reached number eight on the country chart.

Rick Hirsch, songwriter, guitarist and producer, was a founding member of rock group Wet Willie, members of the Alabama Music Hall of Fame. Hirsch, a native of Mobile, now divides his time between Los Angeles and his Studio H2O on Dog River in his hometown. He produced the CD that accompanies this book.

Nall, an Alabama artist who has also worked extensively in Europe, did the cover art for this book and CD. Having grown up in Troy, Alabama, and graduated from the University of Alabama, he later studied under Salvador Dali. His work is on permanent display at the Boston Museum of Fine Arts and the Beaux Arts Museum in Nice, France. He now lives in Fairhope and is currently at work on a portrait of Hank Williams.